BABY'S FIRST
Psychology ABC's

Text and illustrations copyright
©2021 Nicola Donaldson
nicoladonaldson.com

With editing by Chelsea.

ISBN: 9798821254283
Imprint: Independently published.

All rights reserved. No part of this publication may be reproduced, stored in a retrieval system, or transmitted in any form of by any means, electronic, mechanical, photocopying, recording or otherwise without the prior permission in writing from the author.

For Keira

ACTUALIZATION
The reaching of one's full potential and enjoyment of life.

BYSTANDER

Bystander Effect - when individuals assume others will help.

CBT

Cognitive Behavior Therapy is a common type of talk therapy.

DIAGNOSIS
The process of identifying a disease or disorder from symptoms.

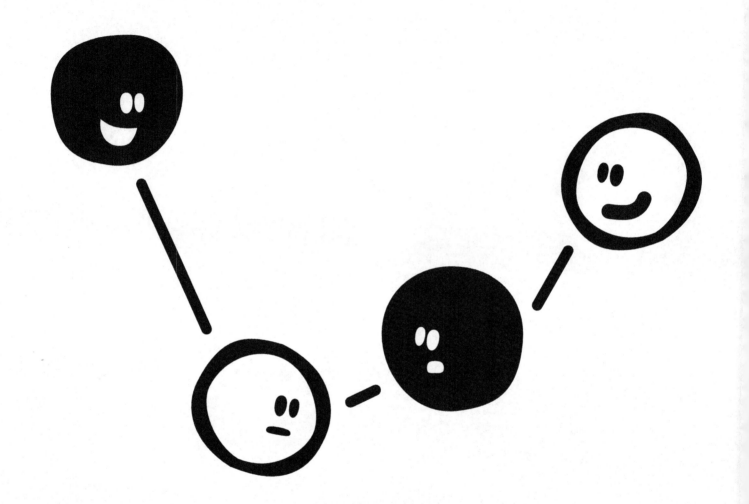

EMOTIONS
A complex feeling-state which influences thought and behavior.

FREUD
Sigmund Freud is considered the founder of psychoanalysis.

GENDER

The sense of being a man, woman, or someone else.

HYPOTHESIS TEST
Using sample data to evaluate claims about a population.

IQ

A number used to infer the relative intelligence of a person.

JUNG
Carl Jung founded analytical psychology, and 'individuation.'

KHOLBERG

Kholberg's theory is how children develop morality in stages.

LIMBIC SYSTEM
The part of a brain involved in behaviors needed for survival.

MEMORY
The process of encoding, storing, and retrieving information.

NEUROSCIENCE
The types of science that study the nervous system and brain.

OPERANT
Operant conditioning is learning via reward and punishment.

PERSONALITY

Thoughts, feelings, and behavior that make someone unique.

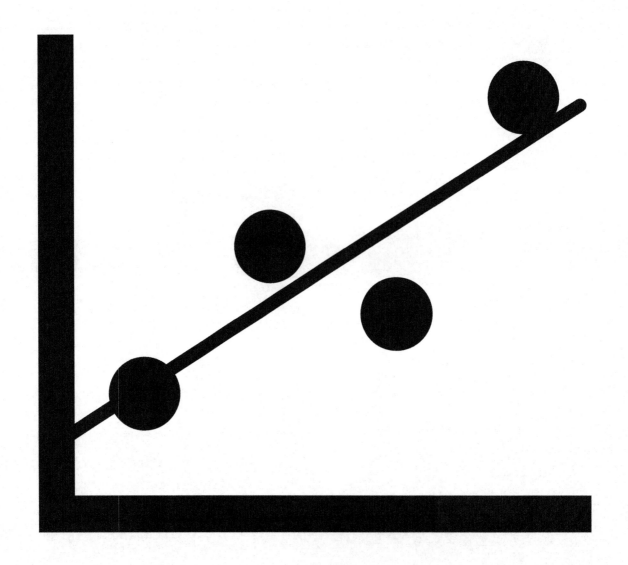

QUANTITATIVE
Research giving numerical data, such as IQ Tests, or Kessler-10.

REINFORCEMENT
Anything that strengthens or increases a behavior.

SELF IMAGE
The view or mental image someone holds of themselves.

TALK THERAPY
A way for clients to work through their thoughts and feelings.

UNCONSCIOUS

Unconscious Bias - social stereotypes held outside awareness.

VALUES

Beliefs that guide what a person views as good, or important.

WADA TEST

Brain functioning is impaired in one hemisphere and compared.

XENOPHOBIA
The fear of strangers, or fear of someone different to themselves.

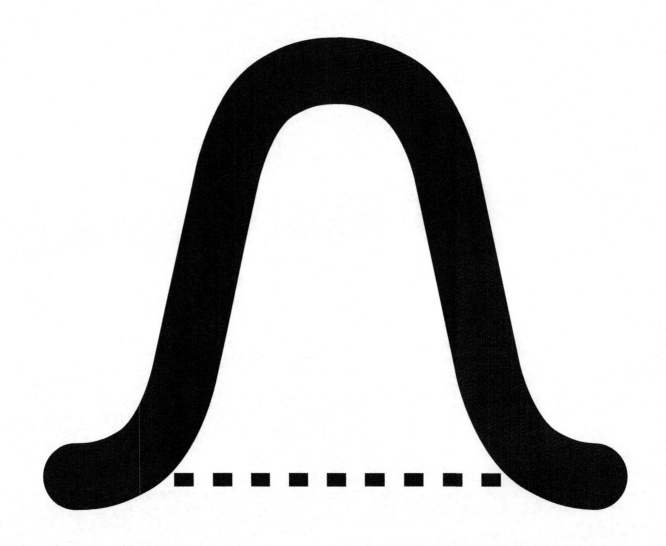

ZIMBARDO
The psychologist who led the famous Stanford Prison Study.

Printed in Great Britain
by Amazon